when the light of any action ceases

poems by

Anne F. Walker

Finishing Line Press
Georgetown, Kentucky

when the light of any action ceases

ACKNOWLEDGMENTS

Some of these poems have been published in *Arrivals and Departures, Classifieds:
An Anthology of Prose Poems, The Muse Apprentice Guild, Janus Head, particulate
matter,* and *Zugernat.*

Previous books of poetry by Anne F. Walker
The Exit Show
Into the Peculiar Dark
Pregnant Poems
Six Months Rent

Poetics: *American Urban Poetics*

Editor: Christen Kincaid

Cover Art: ©Alicia Boal

Author Photo: ©Alicia Boal

Cover Design: Elizabeth Maines

Printed in the USA on acid-free paper.
Order online: www.finishinglinepress.com
          also available on amazon.com

Author inquiries and mail orders:
Finishing Line Press
P. O. Box 1626
Georgetown, Kentucky 40324
U. S. A.

Table of Contents

for my kind, brilliant, and compassionate teacher of poetry and poetics
Alfred Arteaga (1950 – 2008)

eyes endless and chocolate.

your mouth sang *happy birthday* to me like Marilyn Monroe
sang to JFK. but we weren't on tv. we were in a café
and you were eating cheesecake. your soft lips soften me

i could see seeing you every morning
endlessly and never not
being softened by that soft mouth.

my hands were cold when you took them
the day after surgery. fear still in my body.
results yet unknown. and me afraid to be public.

.

Bed Creaks

sometimes for skin
there is no skin for skin
there is a word.

parts of the morning come together as a newborn's skull /
slowly / filling in the gaps / hardening / the addiction to
faith returning

the weather changes to rain.

radiate(.) flowerfields

my body becomes
accustomed to these openings
where your hands radiate
flowerfields on my skin
imperfect

Interstate 5

when 7 she said   . . . *someone repossessed the mountains.*
in the smog

cotton balls line the tumbleweed freeway fallen
off dark burgundy brown sick plants
next to the aqueduct.

looking skyward through a harvest to rowed
red star leaves / on trees
the dust beneath like (light) brown sugar
the sky like blue taffy.

sweet ugly flower

i go through it all 1/2 blind
more than 1/2
running parallel narrations to inform me
on simple on basic on knowledge & magic
& you / can't stop bringing it back to you
like a bad habit or grammar / train marks
softness of a mouth.

air thick & heavy with November *flowers*
your mouth

(or, small leaves imprint sky

it's a balloon inside
how lit i am about you
covered with skin so it's secret

you reach out your hand
pull me in embrace
out in the light

small leaves imprint the sky
i see you and it's not paper or pictures
or memory i see you live

a small hand of flowers

tiny black birds migrate though leafless trees
like desire / men in cafés
or light / conversations which include
the body / somehow include consent

cinco de mayo

as a last clatter of being that ~
scansions changed ~   i fell in.
deeply into satin black like the period
that ends the sentence. creates an opening in which to fall.
you showed me conclusion and i simply
pitched   forward toward

red

bed is still warm from you here. the marks on your shoulder have
    disappeared
under red eddie bauer winter clothes, unlocked back screen, a child
    in the shower

you freckle from the years of sun, water, ocean, inland valley
    spreading suburb
all up and down california   /   your shoulders so often pull in
    close

fill my eyes

you're late

there's a concrete boat in mare channel. three stories high. six
stories high. the fall slip sun retreats off air conditioners and
    windows' slant
on the roof above warehouse windows. trees frame it and crane
after crane lines the water. your face is the moon not yet in the sky.

brittle shell / tricky music

i like the way sound
wraps your home: clear
around yolk / held

by busses, street traffic, a school yard / neighbors walking
on the floor that makes your ceiling creaking

even

the window in your bathroom,
just off-line like a glass slat missing at
the bottom. horizontal light bars   vertical
patches of yellow flowers on the dirt-white draw.
even...it's cold out / even...you open
the window while (we are) wet still

to see you november flower

i dress up in love for you
sister love rock-star love
baby love child love
hands and feet dog and ear
love like your mouth
sweet ugly flower
the world's upside down.

swift unfractioned immaculate

stars,
again the traffic lights skim swift unfractioned immaculate / sigh of
stars,
you are up on stage in paris in sweden in london and lisbon and
     marseilles
you are having not much to say
you play. i send you poems. you play and something between us
     listens.
i wish i could keep it up forever.

but it's the glint of the sword of Damocles suspended there in the
     air by that horsehair. i don't
like to feel it. and mostly, without your touch
the air is cold, i turn. and walk the long halls of this life
barely having known you.

simple-like-that chiasma:

you're laundry; no, not laundry but the sweet tart box
the box of sweet tarts in the rattan basket which holds laundry
    quarters. you seem
afraid i'll catch you. no, that's not exactly it either
maybe afraid i'll catch what you have. a depression. a virus, cold /
    fear or pain.
but really, you just you. then with me, you just two

like in the beginning of Armageddon—
"Houston ...

(i found this this morning)
i don't have one on whose body
        back and forth with my own
        intricacies of intimacies are written.
the time in flesh it needs
the time dressed in kitchens and movie theatres
        and friends' homes
        then turtlenecks slowly unpeeled
to reveal the shining naked skin

i have a thought of you
        and your presence with which i walk
        as if you were the dead
whose memory i carry as heat
        waiting for me the other side
        of the loud crowded foreign river
loud and echoing as in an indoor pool
        with unruly boys
        and families bathed in that light chlorine.

fall all over

on the dark wood cutting board in the window's light
the water is a waterfall at zero gravity. pesto from last night's pizza
washes off it. i can't stop
looking at it. i know i should conserve water in this dry climate. i
    know
you are somewhere ingraining in the air i take in and out of my lungs.

you a part of this landscape of distant hills over square apartments.
trees limning the walk. buzzing of industry all over me.

it's (all) gold

It's not like I want to be here forever. It's just that
we are. The purple water after the sunset. The houses
each different and stones for beach and beachwood and the people
from in the monster truck
searching / for their cell phone / under
branches laid up by surf:

Here we come to the ends of the earth
and it's shaped like a motel room
shaped like inside a boat
and you pour red wine.

52L line up to school

just the edge
of that color
blue under the stick
ing branches

and how could i scratch all the late-night plaza-stops
drunken at the corner / the knowing
so many people in rose apartments adjacent / the walking
through unburied skeletons of just-poured basements
when parts of this neighborhood were
struck from ravine

how could i squeeze that and the deepening purple night like a flower
    for you against
my thigh now like a few words next to you on a bus as we trace like
    color dipped in
blood by some surgeon testing, testing for something in blood (we)
    trace the line up the
slight hill.

Nova Scotia Journal

Stone rubble in patches
like clutter organized inside a mind to sidestep.

Moon a small orange cataract
on a pallid blue eye.

Light belly of the clouds.
The longing waxing and waning gets no better.

Rose

The one room smells like strawberries
from the red candle we've been
burning these last days.

The other smells lightly
like the rose he has brought,
and one purple and yellow flower
he picked tonight after we walked.

He is gone now.

Garden

Sometimes the soft
sausage armed woman

in her thin white dress
over blue polyester checker pants

moves in wild awe of the yard full of rose bushes,
her garden. Not going there often

or controlling anything,
she imagines.

Collage

A small store pushed full of old art and guitars
and books and a saddle, and tin things rust.

Thin straight line of smoke
from a hot knife ash
emptied into the sink full of dishes and pans.

Body the shape of wringing hands.

Startling orange

    White tree arms reach out,
million-finger spray,
      intricacy of
         Queen Anne's lace,
    veins,
neuro-transmitters
hold
    like antennae
secrets back from the dark.

Korona

Steam over black coffee,
threads of cheese cloth laying almost invisibly
down in ink.
Reappear and fold back.

Prose

When the first class bus hit that drunk farmer's tractor stopped in the road it went over. Bent into the ploughed winter fields less than a hundred miles south of Mexico City. Passengers crawled out the windows. The lights were all off. The little VW couldn't see anything until it hit, and exploded in light. My parents said no one moved in the car, but everyone in the field could see them on fire. My father said the bus driver had tried to pull them out. But the heat was too strong. He said the bus driver sat and wept on the fields' edge, and there was nothing to do.

Slice

the niggly thin line today is addiction
to hands to press butt and back to front
to the seated spoon the hanging spoon the side by side
texts and phone calls the hour to hour check-ins
knowing he is just a slim wave away.
across sheets or bed, across pillows or dreams
i call out to you at night still
waking between 4 and 530am
hearing the pacific's waves
and the light from the tower
sweep across ocean
i hear silence
and you thinking

Originally from Berkeley, **Anne F. Walker** grew up in Toronto, Canada. There she began her writing and publishing career, studying with bpNichol, Frank Davey, and Susan Swan while earning a BFA in Creative Writing from York University. She returned to California for her MFA from Mills College. At the University of California, Berkeley she earned her PhD, studying with Alfred Arteaga, Lyn Hejinian, Hertha D. Sweet Wong, and Robert Hass.

Her published collections include *Six Months Rent* (Black Moss Press), *Pregnant Poems* (Black Moss Press), *Into the Peculiar Dark* (The Mercury Press & The bpNichol Foundation), and *The Exit Show* (Palimpsest Press). *American Urban Poetics* is her published poetics book.

She directs the graduate writing program at Holy Names University, Oakland, California.